Dedication

I have met so many amazing people in my journey as a visually impaired chef. Particularly, those who overcame their hesitations and had the courage to start cooking again. I dedicate this book to all of them as well as the team I have worked closely with over the past couple of years; Louise, my eyes when I needed them for the editing of this book, and my RNIB managers, Andrea, Neil, Adam, Danielle and Terri for giving me the confidence to grow.

Thank you

Kim Jaye

Contents

Desserts

Introduction

Twenty-five years ago, I lost a substantial amount of my sight due to an illness. As with everybody that experiences sight loss, I was devastated. I found even the simplest of tasks daunting and seemingly impossible.

Slowly, I began to relearn the simple things that I once took for granted. Such as finding my way around the house without bashing into anything, putting makeup on without smudging it, and most importantly, cooking for my family, my health and my mental wellbeing. Being able to cook made me feel productive and creative.

It was hard at first. There were many mishaps and accidents, but eventually I began to rely more on my other senses. I could smell the aroma of the cumin seeds coming through in the oil in the pan, letting me know it had infused. When cooking on the hob, I could hear whether the dish I was making was too hot just by the sound of the ingredients sizzling. I could tell simply by touching a steak whether it was raw, rare, medium or well-done. And finally, relying on taste to know whether a dish required further seasoning.

Being able to cook through relying on my other senses gave me such confidence. I was able to not just feed my family as I would have done normally, but actually whip up their favourite, comforting dishes. As my confidence grew, I dared to throw my own dinner parties and banquets, sometimes for over a hundred people. I have always liked a challenge!

With the help of RNIB (Royal National Institute of Blind People), I began to impart my knowledge and experience to not only the visually impaired community, but to sighted people too. It was whilst preparing to teach Indian cuisine to a group of amazing VI volunteers that I ventured into writing with my first recipe book *A Taste of Spice'*, an Indian cookery book, with all profits going to RNIB.

During this time, I was often asked for recipes from other cultures. With this in mind, I have developed this recipe book. My advice is to cook with all your senses, whether you are visually impaired or not. It makes for a more immersive experience, improving the success of a dish and furthermore, it is a lot of fun.

Starters

Sour Chicken Wings

Love chicken wings without the hassle of deep frying? Then this simple recipe is for you. Cooked in the oven, these moreish and succulent wings work wonderfully as a starter, but are also great for buffets and barbecues. For a more flavoursome and mouth-watering result, marinating for a minimum of 3 hours is a must.

Ingredients:
- 12 chicken wings
- 100g of cabbage, finely shredded
- 3cm of ginger root, peeled and finely chopped
- 1/4 teaspoon of salt
- 1/4 teaspoon of ground black pepper
- 1/4 teaspoon of ground ginger
- 3 tablespoons of dark brown sugar
- 3 tablespoons of cider vinegar

Method:

1. In a mixing bowl, add the dark brown sugar, cider vinegar, ginger root, ginger powder and the salt and black pepper, mixing thoroughly.
2. Add the chicken wings, rubbing the marinade into the skin thoroughly.
3. Chill this bowl in the fridge for a minimum of 3 hours to marinate.
4. Cook in the oven at 200°C for 25 minutes, or even barbecue - British weather permitting of course!
5. Garnish with the shredded cabbage and serve.

French Onion Soup (V)

This classic soup recipe is always a firm favourite for its delicious caramelised onions, deep and savoury in flavour. This light and delicate dish serves particularly well as a starter before a hearty main course.

Ingredients:
- 50g of butter
- 50ml of crème fraîche or double cream (optional)
- 10 large white onions, peeled and finely sliced
- 4 spring onions, finely chopped (keeping the stems separate from the onion bulb)
- 1 teaspoon of salt
- 1/2 teaspoon of ground black pepper
- 1 tablespoon of olive oil

Method:

1. In a large saucepan, melt the butter and add the olive oil.
2. Add the onions and the spring onion bulbs (setting aside the spring onion stems for later) and fry on a low heat, stirring often.
3. Fry until the onions are medium brown and caramelised. When the onions are stirred, they should clump together, almost as if they are trying to form a ball.
4. Add 1 litre of boiling water as well as the salt and black pepper and boil for 10 minutes.
5. Blitz the soup until smooth.
6. Garnish with the chopped spring onion stems set aside earlier.
7. Add the crème fraiche or double cream just before serving.
8. Serve with bread and butter.

Crab Cakes (VG options)

A fish starter staple, this recipe is simple and easy to make. Garnished with a drizzle of tartar sauce or lemon mayonnaise, this is always a lovely, fresh starter. Alternatively, crab cakes can be used as part of a main dish, with a baked fish on top.

Ingredients:
- 170g of crab meat (for a vegan alternative, use 30g of shredded cabbage, 1/2 a carrot, peeled and finely diced and 50g of non-dairy cheese instead)
- 500ml of milk (for a vegan alternative, use soya milk instead)
- 6 large potatoes, peeled and chopped into 3cm cubes
- 1 teaspoon of parsley, finely chopped
- 1/2 teaspoon of salt
- 1/2 teaspoon of ground black pepper
- 1/4 teaspoon of lemon juice
- 1 tablespoon of olive oil
- 5 slices of white bread, blitzed into breadcrumbs

Method:

1. Put the potatoes into a large saucepan filled with milk over a high heat, ensuring the potatoes are completely covered with the liquid.

2. When the potatoes feel soft, drain and transfer them to a mixing bowl and mash them until you can feel there are no lumps.

3. Add the salt, black pepper, lemon juice, breadcrumbs, parsley and crab meat into the bowl and mix together.

4. Taking a handful of the potato mixture, form into burger-shaped rounds until they feel approximately 2cm thick. Alternatively, you can use a large, round biscuit cutter. At this stage you can freeze the crab cakes for later use if you wish.

5. In a frying pan, add the olive oil and fry the crab cakes on both sides until both sides feel crispy or until they are golden brown in colour. For a healthier option, these can be cooked in the oven at 180°C for 20 minutes instead.

6. Serve with either tartar sauce or lemon mayonnaise and garnish with a leafy salad.

Vegetable Soup (VG)

Is there anything more comforting than home-made soup? This vegetable soup recipe is one of my favourites on a cold winter's day but it is actually great any day of the year. Vegetable soup is so convenient too as you can include any vegetables you wish and it freezes very well. This particular recipe includes penne pasta, allowing it to not only be a starter, but also a hearty lunch.

Ingredients:
- 1 medium carrot, peeled and diced
- 1 small white onion, peeled and finely chopped
- 1 celery stick, diced
- 50g of white cabbage, shredded finely
- 8 fresh basil leaves
- 2 cloves of garlic, peeled and finely chopped
- 1/2 teaspoon of salt
- 1/4 teaspoon of ground black pepper
- 1/2 teaspoon of mixed herbs
- 2 vegetable stock cubes
- A 400g tin of chopped tomatoes
- 20g of dry penne pasta (other pasta may be used)

- 1 tablespoon of olive oil
- 100ml of red wine (optional)

Method:

1. Bring a large saucepan to heat and add the olive oil, garlic and mixed herbs, heating for 15 seconds or until you can smell the garlic coming through in the oil.
2. Add the onions and cook for 5 minutes on a medium heat. You should be able to feel the texture of the onions go from hard to soft.
3. Add the carrot, celery stick and cabbage and sauté for 5 minutes.
4. Crumble the stock cubes into 1 litre of boiling water and stir until dissolved.
5. Add the stock liquid, the chopped tomatoes and the salt and black pepper in with the vegetables.
6. Add the red wine and tear the basil leaves into the soup and simmer for a further 10 minutes.
7. Add the pasta and boil for 15 minutes or until the pasta feels soft.
8. Taste and add more seasonings if necessary.
9. Serve with bread and butter.

Chargrilled Mackerel with Pickled Beetroot

Fresh mackerel and pickled beetroot are a heavenly combination. This impressive dish is made in stages, pickling the beetroot and then marinating and cooking the mackerel. Admittedly, it is a little time consuming, but well worth the effort.

Ingredients:

- 3 fresh mackerels, deboned and filleted
- 100g of crème fraîche
- 500g of raw beetroot, peeled
- 3 teaspoons of chives, finely chopped
- 1cm of ginger root, peeled and finely chopped
- 1/2 a teaspoon of ground black pepper
- 3 teaspoons of black sesame seeds, toasted
- 1 teaspoon of wasabi (or horseradish)
- 100g of clear honey
- 100ml of red wine vinegar
- 2 teaspoons of soy sauce
- 1 teaspoon of sesame oil
- 1 teaspoon of extra virgin olive oil

Method:
1. Mix the honey, red wine vinegar, black pepper and 120ml of water in a medium saucepan, listening until you can hear it boil.
2. Once boiled, transfer to a mixing bowl and leave to cool.
3. Fill another saucepan with hot water and add the beetroot and cook until it feels soft.
4. Drain the beetroot and run it under cold water.
5. Slice the beetroot into thin rounds.
6. Add the beetroot to the cooled pickling liquid in the mixing bowl and chill overnight in the fridge, for a minimum of 12 hours.
7. The next day, brush the mackerel with soy sauce and leave to marinate for 45 minutes.
8. Whisk together the wasabi and the crème fraîche and season to taste.
9. Brush the sesame oil onto a wire rack grill, placed on top of an oven tray.
10. Put the mackerel on top of the wire rack with the scales facing up and grill on high.
11. Grill the fish for 3 minutes until the scales are charred and you can smell the smokiness.

12. On a serving plate, finely spread the wasabi and crème fraiche mixture into a 12cm circle (approximately the size of a CD) in the centre of the plate.
13. On top of this, remove the beetroot from the pickling liquid and arrange on top.
14. Scatter the ginger, toasted black sesame seeds and chives on top.
15. Arrange the mackerel on top of the beetroot and drizzle with the olive oil.

Asian Battered Cod (VG options)

This recipe is a twist on the traditional battered fish we all know and love, but tantalisingly spiced. The batter made in this dish can be used for a variety of foods, which is ideal if you want to make this dish vegetarian or vegan friendly. As a vegetarian myself, I substitute the cod for Paneer (an Indian cheese that doesn't melt) but this batter also works well with sliced potatoes, cauliflower or even onion rings.

Ingredients:
- 1 small cod or any whitefish such as halibut or hake, deboned and cut into 3cm chunks (for a vegetarian alternative, use Paneer cheese, or for a vegan alternative, use vegetables instead)
- 100ml of milk (for a vegan alternative, use soya milk instead)
- 1 egg, beaten (this can be omitted for vegans)
- A 60g bunch of fresh coriander, finely chopped
- 3/4 teaspoon of salt
- 1/2 teaspoon of ground black pepper

- 1/2 teaspoon of chilli powder (this can be substituted for smoked paprika if you're not a fan of spices)
- 200g of plain flour
- 1/2 a teaspoon of bicarbonate of soda
- 1/2 a teaspoon of lemon juice
- 3 tablespoons of tomato purée
- Vegetable oil in a deep-fat fryer

Method:

1. In a mixing bowl, add the plain flour, bicarbonate of soda, salt, ground black pepper and chilli powder.
2. Add the egg, tomato purée, coriander, lemon juice and half the milk and mix together.
3. Slowly add the remaining half of the milk, mixing until the batter is smooth. When you dip a spoon into it, the mixture should coat the spoon whilst still dripping off it. If the batter is too thick, add more milk. If the batter is too liquid, add more flour.
4. Set aside the batter for 45 minutes.
5. Heat the vegetable oil in a deep-fat fryer. When you can smell the oil, gently drop a teaspoon of batter into it. The oil is ready for

frying when you are able to hear the batter bubbling and rising to the surface.

6. Dip the fish (or Paneer or vegetables) into the batter, ensuring it is fully coated.

7. Very gently, place in the hot oil using tongs.

8. Fry until golden-brown in colour or until the batter feels and sounds crispy when you remove it from the oil and touch it with a utensil.

9. When removing the battered cod from the oil, put them onto a piece of kitchen roll to absorb the excess grease.

10. When you have removed all of the battered cod from the oil, the bubbling noise of the oil should be reduced significantly. If you can still hear this noise, it is likely there is still cod or loose batter present in the oil.

11. Serve with slices of fresh lemon and either tartar sauce or lemon mayonnaise.

Seared Lemon Scallops (VG options)

Tasty and refreshing, this modern dish is normally reserved for fancy restaurants but it is actually so easy and quick to make at home. A perfect starter for a special occasion, these scallops are divinely buttery with a lovely zesty kick.

Ingredients:
- 6 scallops, chopped in half (for a vegan alternative, use potato slices instead)
- 30g of butter - for frying the greens (for a vegan alternative, use non-dairy butter instead)
- 50g of butter - for frying the scallops
- 10 cabbage leaves or a bunch of kale, roughly chopped
- 6 cherry tomatoes
- 10 fresh tarragon leaves
- 1 clove of garlic, peeled and finely chopped
- 1/4 teaspoon of salt
- 1/4 teaspoon of ground black pepper
- The zest of a lemon
- 1 teaspoon of lemon juice
- 1 tablespoon of olive oil

Method:

1. In a frying pan, add 30g of butter and heat until the butter has melted.
2. Add the cabbage or kale and fry until softened.
3. Add the salt, black pepper and the cherry tomatoes.
4. In another frying pan, add 50g of butter and the olive oil and heat until the butter has melted.
5. Add the garlic, tarragon and lemon zest and cook for 15 seconds or until you smell the aromas coming through in the oil.
6. Add the scallops and cook for 2 minutes on both sides.
7. Add the lemon juice and cook for a further 20 seconds on both sides.
8. Plate the cabbage and cherry tomatoes, placing the scallops on top.

Duck Liver on Toast with Onion Chutney (VG options)

This indulgent dish, rich and full of flavour is most definitely a luxurious starter, perfect for a dinner party. Due to the way it is plated, it also serves well as a tasty appetiser when you're really out to impress.

Ingredients:
- 400g of duck liver (for a vegan alternative, use blitzed mushrooms or blitzed vegan Quorn fillets instead)
- 50g of butter (for a vegan alternative, use non-dairy butter instead)
- 5 large red onions, peeled and finely chopped
- 1/4 teaspoon of salt
- 1/4 teaspoon of black pepper
- 1 tablespoon of dark muscovado sugar
- 2 tablespoons of cider vinegar
- 1 baguette sliced into rounds

Method:
1. Place a pan on the heat and cook the red onions for 5 minutes.
2. Add the muscovado sugar and the cider vinegar, cooking for further 5 minutes.
3. Transfer this chutney to a bowl and chill in the fridge.
4. Heat the butter in a frying pan until you can hear the butter sizzling.
5. Add the duck livers and fry for 5 minutes.
6. Leave the duck livers to cool for 10 minutes.
7. Place the duck livers into a food processor and blitz until they become a smooth paste.
8. Transfer the duck livers to a mixing bowl and add the salt and black pepper.
9. Chill in the fridge for at least 3 hours.
10. Lightly toast the baguette slices on the grill.
11. Spread the duck liver pâté onto the baguette slices.
12. Serve with the red onion chutney on the side (or on top if you are making appetisers).

Lime Whitebait

These tiny, silvery members of the herring group always work well as a starter. This particular recipe uses lime to create a refreshing, yet sharp dish, perfect as a starter or even as a meal in its own right.

Ingredients:
- 900g of whitebait
- 2 limes cut into thick wedges
- The zest of 2 limes
- 2 teaspoons of parsley, finely chopped
- 1/4 teaspoon of salt
- 1/4 teaspoon of ground black pepper
- 200g of plain flour
- 1/4 teaspoon of sesame seeds
- 2 tablespoons of vegetable oil

Method:
1. Put the flour, parsley, lime zest, sesame seeds and the salt and black pepper into a bowl and mix together.
2. Put the whitebait into this mixture ensuring it is well-coated.
3. In a frying pan, add the vegetable oil and heat until you can hear the oil bubbling.
4. Fry the whitebait in the hot oil until golden-brown in colour or until the exterior feels crispy.
5. Remove the whitebait from the pan and place onto a piece of kitchen roll to absorb the excess oil.
6. Squeeze the lime wedges on to the whitebait and serve with a leafy salad and tartar sauce.

Paprika Chicken (VG options)

Paprika chicken is an effortless starter that is so easy to make. What makes this dish successful is allowing it time to marinate, creating a deliciously juicy dish with the heightened flavour of the aromatic and fragrant combination of spices.

Ingredients:

- 4 skinned chicken thighs, skin removed (for a vegan alternative, use vegan Quorn fillets instead)
- A 500g tub of Greek yoghurt (for a vegan alternative, use non-dairy yoghurt instead)
- 3/4 teaspoon of salt
- 1/4 teaspoon of ground black pepper
- 1/4 teaspoon of chilli powder (omit or use more depending on your taste)
- 4 teaspoons of smoked paprika powder
- 2 teaspoons of barbecue seasoning powder
- 1 teaspoon of lemon juice
- 1 tablespoon of tomato purée
- 1 tablespoon of vegetable oil

Method:
1. Cut shallow slits into the chicken or Quorn.
2. In a mixing bowl, put all the other ingredients together and mix thoroughly.
3. Place the chicken into the mixing bowl and rub the marinade into the chicken thoroughly, especially the slits.
4. Put this bowl in the fridge for a minimum of 12 hours to marinate, preferably 24 hours though.
5. Cook in the oven at 180°C for 35 minutes until cooked through.
6. Garnish with a leafy salad and serve.

Beef Crostini

A perfect marriage of beef and horseradish, this is an exquisite, full-flavoured dish that is so simple to make. Beef crostini works lovely as a starter or even as a dinner party appetiser.

Ingredients:
- 800g of beef fillet
- 250g of Stilton, sliced into thin wedges
- 250ml of crème fraîche
- 50g of mixed leaf salad
- 2 tablespoons of chives, finely chopped
- 1/4 teaspoon of salt
- 1/4 teaspoon of ground black pepper
- 1/2 teaspoon of cracked black pepper
- 1 teaspoon of English mustard powder
- 1 teaspoon of horseradish sauce
- 1 teaspoon of olive oil
- 1 baguette, sliced into rounds

Method:

1. Rub the beef with the olive oil and mustard powder, seasoning with salt and ground black pepper.
2. Heat a pan on the hob at medium heat and place the beef into the pan, cooking for 2 minutes on each side until the flesh has seared.
3. Place the beef in a baking tray and put it in the oven at 180°C for 10 minutes for it to be cooked rare, or 14 minutes for it to be cooked medium.
4. Remove the beef from the oven and cover it with the olive oil. Leave it to rest for 20 minutes.
5. Mix together the crème fraiche, horseradish, cracked black pepper and chives.
6. Slice the beef finely.
7. Lightly toast the sliced baguette on the grill.
8. When lightly toasted, remove the baguette and arrange the mixed leaf salad on top, adding a few splodges of the crème fraiche mixture.
9. Place the slices of beef on top of this with the Stilton placed on top.

10. Add a little more of the crème fraiche mixture to finish and serve.

Herb Butters

Most recipes ask for fresh herbs, giving extra taste and aroma. I don't know about you, but I always find I have lots of leftover herbs from the too large packets that are sold in the supermarkets. In my kitchen, very little goes to waste, so whenever I do have any herbs left over, I make herb butter and store it in handy individual portions in my freezer.

Ingredients:
- 250g of butter
- 60g of your herb of choice, finely chopped

Method:
1. Let the butter come to room temperature so that it is easier to mix.
2. Choose one herb (such as parsley or tarragon etc), and when it has been finely chopped, mix it with the butter.
3. Once well mixed, put the herb butter into ice cube trays and freeze. I personally like an ice cube tray with a silicone base so that it is easier to pop the herb cube out.

Main Courses

Steak

In the kitchen, I love the technology designed to support individuals with visual impairment. I have benefitted from a number of these devices, everything from talking weighing scales, talking microwaves, talking label readers, liquid level indicators etc. You name it, I've got it. These days, even talking thermometers are available, but when I am cooking steak, I am old school.

In my opinion, the best way to check that a steak is cooked to your preference is through touch. Although using a thermometer would give you a precise temperature reading, the process pierces the meat, letting all the juices run out, resulting in a less juicy and less flavoursome steak. Most decent chefs use this touch technique too so you're in good company.

So how do you check on a steak's doneness by touch? It is easy, all you need is your hands.

Raw Steak – With your left hand open and relaxed, with the palm facing upwards, use the index finger from your right hand to feel your left hand's palm in the area just below the thumb. It should feel very fleshy and this is what raw steak feels like.

Rare Steak – On your left hand, bring your thumb to your index finger so that they touch and then touch the same area of your palm again with the index finger of your right hand. You should notice that it is slightly firmer, yet still somewhat spongy. This is the texture of rare steak.

Medium-Rare Steak – Bring your thumb to your middle finger and touch the same area of your palm again. Again, this should feel even firmer and this is what medium-rare steak feels like.

Medium Steak – Bring your thumb to your ring finger and touch the same area of your palm again. This will feel even more taut, replicating the firmness of medium cooked steak.

Well-Done Steak – Bring your thumb to your little finger and you will notice the palm area feels taut and firm. This is an indication of what a well-done steak feels like when you press on it. Compare this to the first open palm position of raw steak and feel the difference.

Asparagus & Pepper Quiche (V)

Although I understand the convenience of them, I don't particularly like the mass-produced supermarket quiches with their bland taste and stodgy consistency. This recipe, with its light and fluffy texture, packed with subtle and complimentary flavours, you'll never want to go back to the supermarket quiche again. Perfect as a main course, the quiche also works well as a lunch, or even as mini quiches for a picnic in the park.

Ingredients:
- A 320g packet of ready-rolled shortcrust pastry (one sheet)
- 6 large eggs, with the yolks and whites separated
- 20g of butter
- 100g of mature Cheddar cheese, grated
- 20g of Mozzarella, grated
- 1 red pepper, finely sliced
- 8 asparagus
- 1 clove of garlic, peeled and finely chopped
- 1/2 teaspoon of mixed herbs
- Salt - for seasoning
- Ground black pepper - for seasoning

Method:
1. Take the pastry out of the fridge to climatize to room temperature so that it is easy to unroll without it breaking.
2. Prepare a 20cm pie dish by greasing it with a thin layer of butter on the base and sides.
3. Gently unroll the pastry over the dish, pressing down the edges and cutting off most of the excess.
4. Chill the pie base in the fridge for 30 minutes.
5. Cut the tips of the asparagus off so that they measure 2cm and set them aside.
6. With the rest of asparagus, chop them up finely and set them aside separately from the asparagus tips.
7. In a saucepan, melt the butter and add the garlic and the mixed herbs, frying for 30 seconds.
8. Now add the sliced peppers and the chopped asparagus stems (not the tips) in the saucepan and fry them on a low heat for 5 minutes.
9. Set the mixture aside to cool slightly.

10. In a mixing bowl, add the egg whites and a pinch of salt and black pepper and whisk until soft peaks form.
11. Very gently, fold in the beaten egg yolks with a spoon into this same bowl.
12. Take the pie dish out of the fridge and sprinkle a layer of the asparagus and pepper mixture at the bottom. Then add a layer of both cheeses and a layer of the egg mixture. Keep repeating the layers until the dish can fill no more.
13. Sprinkle the top with the asparagus tips set aside earlier.
14. Cook in the oven at 170°C for 35 minutes.
15. After 35 minutes, check to see if the quiche is done by feeling the top. The top should feel firm. Also, pierce the centre of the quiche with a knife. If the knife comes out clean, the quiche is done.
16. Cut into large slices and serve with a leafy salad, coleslaw and new potatoes.

Chicken Rosé (VG options)

Perfect for a cosy night in, chicken rosé is a delicious, hearty meal. It is one of my favourite comfort dishes, perfect for cold winter's night. For me, Quorn works wonderfully in this dish, as like the chicken, it soaks up all the juices and flavours of all the other ingredients.

Ingredients:
- 2 chicken breasts, skinned (for a vegan alternative, use vegan Quorn fillets instead)
- 1 onion, sliced into rings
- 7 button mushrooms, sliced
- 8 pickled onions
- 8 rosemary leaves
- 3 cloves of garlic, peeled and finely chopped
- Salt - for seasoning
- Ground black pepper - for seasoning
- 600ml of chicken gravy
- 1 teaspoon of mixed herbs
- 1 teaspoon of vegetable oil
- 200ml of red wine

Method:

1. In a large frying pan, heat up the vegetable oil, mixed herbs and the garlic and cook for 20 seconds until you can smell the garlic in coming through in the oil.
2. Add the chicken breasts (or Quorn), frying for 6 minutes on one side and then 4 minutes on the other. The pan should be hot enough for you to be able to hear it sizzle.
3. Add the mushrooms, onions and half the red wine, cooking for a further 5 minutes.
4. Add the gravy, rosemary leaves, the remaining half of the red wine, pickled onions and season with salt and black pepper and simmer for 5 minutes.
5. Transfer to a casserole dish and cover with foil or a lid.
6. Cook in the oven at 180°C for approximately 25 minutes.
7. Serve with potatoes and seasonal vegetables.

Stuffed Moroccan Aubergines (VG options)

Stuffed aubergines are a popular dish in Morocco and it's not difficult to see why. With its rich, unique flavour, aubergines work best when coupled with other full-bodied foods such as those included in this recipe. As aubergines are so distinctive in texture and flavour, they may not be to everybody's taste. If this is the case, this recipe also works nicely where peppers are used as the vessel.

Ingredients:
- 100g of lean lamb mince (for a vegan alternative, use soya mince instead)
- 30g of mature Cheddar, grated (for a vegan alternative, use non-dairy cheese instead)
- 10g of Mozzarella, grated (omit if vegan)
- 40g of butter (for a vegan alternative, use non-dairy butter instead)
- 2 large aubergines
- 30g of mushrooms, finely chopped
- 1 green pepper, finely chopped
- 30g of frozen sweetcorn
- 8 basil leaves

- 3 cloves of garlic, peeled and finely chopped
- 1/2 teaspoon of salt
- 1/2 teaspoon of ground black pepper
- 1/4 teaspoon of chilli powder
- 1/4 teaspoon of ground cinnamon
- 1 teaspoon of Cajun powder
- 2 teaspoons of smoked paprika
- 1 teaspoon of cumin seeds
- A 400g tin of chopped tomatoes
- 30g of tinned chickpeas
- 100g of plain flour
- 1 tablespoon of olive oil
- 50ml of red wine

Method:

1. In a mixing bowl, add the plain flour, butter and a pinch of salt. Rub the butter into the flour using your fingers until you feel that it resembles fine breadcrumbs and then put to one side.
2. Slice the aubergines in half lengthways and hollow out the centre carefully without cutting into the sides. Chop the scooped-out aubergine into small pieces and set aside.

3. In a saucepan, heat up the olive oil and add the cumin seeds.
4. When you can smell the cumin coming through the oil, add the garlic and cook for 1 minute.
5. Add the mince and cook for 5 minutes.
6. Add the previously scooped-out aubergine (set aside earlier) as well as the mushrooms, chickpeas and the green pepper and cook for another 5 minutes.
7. Add the sweetcorn, salt, black pepper, chilli powder, cinnamon, Cajun and smoked paprika and cook a further 5 minutes.
8. Add the tinned tomatoes, red wine and half the basil leaves, cooking for 10 minutes.
9. Add the remaining basil and set aside.
10. Place a layer of the mince mixture into the aubergine and then a layer of both cheeses.
11. Continue filling up the aubergine with layers of mince and cheese, building it up until it fills it completely.
12. Sprinkle the breadcrumb mixture on top and cook in the oven at 180°C for 40 minutes.
13. Serve with rice.

Stuffed Cabbage Rolls (V)

Stuffed full of hearty ingredients, these cabbage rolls are packed with plenty of tasty vegetables, rich in vitamins and nutrients. Served with rice, this works lovely as a main course but can also be served as a side dish too.

Ingredients:
- 50g of butter
- 50g of mature Cheddar cheese, grated
- 50g of Mozzarella, grated
- 6 white cabbage leaves
- 150g of mixed mushrooms, sliced
- 50g of frozen sweetcorn
- 1 green pepper, finely chopped
- 8 black olives, sliced in halves
- 7 basil leaves
- 3 cloves of garlic, peeled and finely chopped
- Salt - for seasoning
- Ground black pepper - for seasoning
- 1 teaspoon of mixed herbs
- 2 400g tins of chopped tomatoes
- 1/2 a mug of basmati rice
- 6 drops of truffle oil

- 1 tablespoon of olive oil
- 100ml of red wine

Method:

1. Fill a large saucepan with hot water. Very gently, place the cabbage leaves into it, trying not to break the leaves.
2. Boil the cabbage for 8 minutes.
3. After 8 minutes, carefully drain the water and set the cabbage aside.
4. Rinse the rice under cold running water for at least 5 minutes in order to rinse the starch off the rice so that it is light and fluffy.
5. Put the rice in a large saucepan and fill it with water and a pinch of salt.
6. Bring the rice to boil and then reduce the heat and place a lid on the pan.
7. Cook for 12 minutes. Don't stir the rice during this time (as this will reactivate the starch).
8. After 12 minutes, check to see that the rice is soft. When it is done, drain away the water and set the rice aside.
9. In a large frying pan, add the butter and half the garlic, cooking for 30 seconds.

10. Then add the mushrooms and sweetcorn and fry for 4 minutes.
11. Add the rice to the mixture as well as the truffle oil and fry for 7 minutes.
12. Very gently, lay a cabbage leaf on a plate and spoon the mixture into the centre of the leaf.
13. Then roll up the cabbage leaf until it resembles a Swiss roll.
14. Place the cabbage rolls into a roasting dish with the seam side down.
15. Repeat the process for the other cabbage leaves and chill the roasting dish in the fridge.
16. In a large saucepan, heat the olive oil and add the remaining half of the garlic as well as the mixed herbs.
17. Add the green pepper and cook for 5 minutes.
18. Add the tins of tomatoes, sliced olives, basil leaves, red wine and season with salt and black pepper, cooking for 10 minutes.
19. Pour the sauce over the cabbage leaves and sprinkle with both of the cheeses.
20. Cook in the oven at 180°C for 20 minutes.
21. Serve with potatoes and seasonal vegetables.

Chicken Cote (VG options)

This is a classic dish, rich in flavours and aromas and so indulgently creamy. You can serve this with wild rice and/or asparagus on the side, or sometimes even with pasta to make it even more of a substantial, hearty meal.

Ingredients:
- 2 skinned chicken breasts (for a vegan alternative, use vegan Quorn fillets instead)
- A 400ml carton of double cream (for a vegan alternative, use non-dairy cream instead)
- 50g of butter (for a vegan alternative, use non-dairy butter instead)
- 200g of sliced mushrooms
- 12 tarragon leaves
- 7 strands of saffron
- 1 clove of garlic, peeled and finely chopped
- 1/2 teaspoon of salt
- 1/2 teaspoon of black pepper
- 1 tablespoon of olive oil
- 5 drops of truffle oil (optional)
- 100ml of white wine

Method:

1. Heat a frying pan and when hot, add the butter and the olive oil.
2. When the butter has melted, add the chopped garlic and fry for 20 seconds.
3. Add the chicken breasts and cook for 5 minutes on one side, then turn the chicken over and cook the other side for 5 minutes too.
4. Add half of the tarragon leaves.
5. When the exterior of the chicken starts to firm up, add the mushrooms and cook for a further 5 minutes.
6. Turn the heat up and add the white wine and carry on cooking until all the liquid has gone and it is sizzling less.
7. Turn the heat down to low and pour in the double cream and add the saffron strands, salt and black pepper.
8. Add five drops of truffle oil and the remaining tarragon leaves.
9. Serve with wild rice and vegetables.

Lamb Tajine (VG options)

Becoming increasingly popular, tajine is a dish so synonymous with the clay pot that it is cooked in, it is actually named after it. A tajine pot is perfectly designed as it seals in the flavours of the ingredients and allows for self-basting by how the moisture rises with nowhere to escape, and so, drips back down over the ingredients again. Thankfully for those of us who do not own a tajine, these results can be replicated with a simple lidded casserole dish.

Quite often, people are daunted by the amount of different spices in this meal, so if you want to make life a little easier, use garam masala powder in place of cloves, cinnamon, cumin, coriander and cardamom as it incorporates all of these.

Ingredients:

- 1kg boneless lamb, diced (for a vegan alternative, use vegan Quorn fillets instead, but please note, adjust the cooking time to 30 minutes less when doing this)
- 5 carrots, peeled and chopped into slices

- 2 medium brown onions, peeled and finely chopped
- The zest of a lemon
- 3 cloves of garlic, peeled and finely chopped
- 1cm of ginger root, peeled and finely chopped
- 1 pinch of saffron
- 1 teaspoon of salt
- 1/4 teaspoon of ground black pepper
- 1/2 teaspoon of ginger powder
- 1/4 teaspoon of turmeric powder
- 1/2 teaspoon of ground cumin
- 1/2 teaspoon of ground coriander
- 1/4 teaspoon of ground cloves
- The seeds of 1 green cardamom pod
- 1 teaspoon of ground cinnamon
- 2 teaspoons of paprika powder
- 2 tablespoons of tomato purée
- 2 tablespoons of clear honey
- 3 tablespoons of cornflour
- 1 lamb stock cube
- 2 tablespoons of olive oil - for the marinade
- 1 tablespoon of olive oil - for cooking the meat

Method:
1. In a mixing bowl, combine the saffron, salt, black pepper, ginger powder, turmeric, cumin, cloves, cardamom seeds, cinnamon, coriander, paprika and the two tablespoons of olive oil and mix well.
2. Add the lamb to the mixing bowl, ensuring it is well coated in the marinade.
3. Put this bowl in the fridge for a minimum of 24 hours to marinate.
4. In a large saucepan, heat one tablespoon of olive oil over a medium heat.
5. Add the lamb and cook the outer flesh until it has browned and sealed and then set this aside.
6. Into the empty pan, add the onions and the carrots and cook for 5 minutes, stirring in the chopped garlic and ginger.
7. Cook for a further 5 minutes until the onion starts to feel softer to the touch.
8. Place the browned lamb into this pan with the zest of the lemon. Also add the tomato purée, honey, cornflour and the stock cube (made up with 400ml of boiling water).

9. Once you can hear the pan starting to boil, reduce the heat to low and put a lid on the pan, allowing it to simmer for 30 minutes.
10. Transfer the contents of the pan into a lidded casserole dish and cook in the oven at 120°C for approximately 1 – 2 hours. You will know when the lamb is done when you can easily cut it with the side of a fork. I always check the lamb every 20 minutes as every lamb is different.
11. Serve on a bed of rice.

Scrumpy Pork

Pork and apple are a traditional pairing for good reason, they are match made in flavour heaven. The savoury taste of the pork being contrasted by the sweetness and tartness of the apple makes this a delicious recipe.

Ingredients:
- 6 pork chops
- 50g of butter
- 2 Granny Smith apples
- 2 sprigs of rosemary
- 1 clove of garlic, peeled and finely chopped
- 1/2 teaspoon of salt
- 1/2 teaspoon of ground black pepper
- 1 vegetable stock cube
- 1 tablespoon of cornflour
- 1 teaspoon of vegetable oil
- 100ml of scrumpy cider

Method:
1. In a large frying pan, heat up the butter and the vegetable oil until you can feel that the butter has melted.

2. Add the pork chops, frying for 5 minutes on one side and then 4 minutes on the other.
3. Add the garlic and cook for 2 minutes.
4. Add the stock cube (dissolved in 100ml of water), rosemary and the scrumpy cider.
5. Bring the liquid to the boil by listening to when it starts to bubble energetically. When it reaches this stage, reduce the heat to a gentle simmer.
6. Peel and core the apples, reserving two ring slices for garnishing later, and slicing the remaining into segments. To avoid the apple rings browning through exposure to the air, put them into a mixing bowl full of cold water and one tablespoon of lemon juice.
7. Add the apple segments into the pan as well as the salt and pepper. Add more stock or cider if necessary.
8. Cook until the pork is tender.
9. Mix two tablespoons of water with the cornflour and then add it to the pan.
10. Serve with mashed potatoes and the remaining apple rings to garnish.

Beef Fillet with Shallot Jus & Caramelised Red Cabbage

This simple beef dish makes for an impressive main served at a dinner party. The caramelised red cabbage is divine and compliments this robust meat beautifully.

Ingredients:
- 1/2 red cabbage, finely sliced
- 2 large shallots, finely chopped
- 1 thyme sprig
- 1 clove of garlic, peeled and finely chopped
- 1/2 teaspoon of salt
- 1/4 teaspoon of ground black pepper
- 1 beef stock cube
- 2 tablespoons of muscovado sugar
- 25ml of sherry vinegar
- 4 tablespoons of red wine vinegar
- 1 tablespoon of olive oil
- 100ml of sweet red wine

Method:

1. In a saucepan, add the red cabbage, muscovado sugar, red wine vinegar, salt and black pepper and cook until the cabbage has softened. Set aside to cool and serve later.
2. To create the shallot jus, put the olive oil, shallots and garlic into a saucepan to cook for 8 minutes on medium heat until the shallots feel soft to the touch.
3. Add the thyme sprig and the sherry vinegar, cooking for another 5 minutes until you can feel and hear that the liquid has evaporated.
4. Add the red wine and reduce the liquid again until most of it has evaporated.
5. Add the beef stock cube (made up with 400ml of boiling water) to the saucepan and cook for a further 15 – 20 minutes.
6. Take the pan off the heat and leave aside, removing and discarding the thyme sprigs.
7. Lightly brush the beef fillets with olive oil and season with salt and black pepper.
8. Put the beef fillets into a hot frying pan, cooking on both sides for 3 – 4 minutes, until the flesh has seared.

9. Put the beef fillets on a roasting tray and cook in the oven at 180ºC for 20 minutes. This length of time will cook the meat until it is rare/medium. Adjust the cooking time if you prefer your meat well-done.
10. Take the beef out of the oven and rest for a further 20 minutes.
11. Heat the shallot jus until it is hot.
12. Place the beef fillets on a plate with the caramelised cabbage, drizzling with the shallot jus.

Cheese & Onion Pie (V)

This book wouldn't be complete without my ultimate cheese and onion pie recipe. This is my go-to comfort food as it is so hearty and satisfying. The key to this recipe is using more than one type of cheese, giving it a real depth of flavour and making it a must for all cheese lovers.

Ingredients:

- 1 large white onion, peeled and finely sliced
- 150g of mature Cheddar cheese, grated
- 100g of Cheshire cheese, grated
- 50g of Red Leicester cheese, grated
- 150g of white Stilton, grated
- 50g of Mozzarella, grated
- A 320g packet of ready-rolled shortcrust pastry (one sheet)
- A 320g packet of ready-rolled puff pastry (one sheet)
- 1 egg, beaten - for the egg wash
- Salt - for seasoning
- Ground black pepper - for seasoning

Method:
1. Take the pastry out of the fridge to climatize to room temperature so that it is easy to unroll without it breaking.
2. Prepare a 20cm pie dish by greasing it with a thin layer of butter on the base and sides.
3. Gently unroll the shortcrust pastry over the dish, pressing down the edges and leaving a 2cm overhang.
4. Chill the pie dish in the fridge.
5. Put a saucepan of hot water on to boil and add the onion slices, cooking for 15 minutes until they feel soft.
6. Drain the onions and season them with salt and black pepper. Set aside to cool.
7. Take the pie dish out of the fridge and add the cheeses in layers, adding the onions throughout. Carry on layering until the pie dish is full and slightly raised above the sides of the dish.
8. Gently unroll the puff pastry sheet on top of the pie.
9. Crimp the pie lid to the edges of the pie using the back of a fork to press the edges together.

10. If there is any pasty left, decorate the top.
11. Using a knife, put a slit in the middle of the top of the pie to allow steam to escape.
12. Chill in the fridge for at least 20 minutes.
13. Brush the pastry top with the beaten egg.
14. Bake in the oven at 170°C for 30 minutes until golden brown.
15. Serve with potatoes and seasonal vegetables.

Artichoke Pie (V)

Due to its variability of fillings, a pie really allows you to get creative with many different ingredient variations. This particular recipe combines artichoke, spinach, mushroom and cheese to create an ever so slightly upmarket pie, definitely worthy of prime of place at a dinner party.

Ingredients:

- 200g of spinach, chopped
- 1 small brown onion, peeled and finely chopped
- 150g of mixed mushrooms, sliced
- 130g of mature Cheddar cheese, grated
- 100ml of milk
- 30g of butter
- A 320g packet of ready-rolled shortcrust pastry (one sheet)
- 2 eggs, beaten - for the mixture
- 1 egg, beaten - for the egg wash
- 1 clove of garlic, peeled and finely chopped
- A 200g jar of artichokes, roughly chopped
- 2 tablespoons of plain flour
- 1 tablespoon of olive oil

Method:

1. Take the pastry out of the fridge to climatize to room temperature so that it is easy to unroll without it breaking.
2. In a saucepan, heat the butter and olive oil until the butter has melted.
3. Add the onion and the garlic and cook for 5 minutes until soft.
4. Stir in the flour, cooking for a further 3 minutes.
5. Gradually stir in the milk until you have a thick sauce. The sauce should leave a coating on a spoon. If it doesn't, add a little more flour.
6. Take the pan off the heat and add the spinach and the artichoke, ensuring it is well coated in the sauce.
7. Stir in the Cheddar and the two beaten eggs and season.
8. Set aside and leave to cool.
9. Prepare a 15cm pie dish by greasing it with a thin layer of butter on the base and sides.
10. Roll out 2/3 of the pastry onto a floured work surface/board until it is approximately 3mm thick.

11. Gently put the pastry over the dish, pressing down the edges and leaving a 2cm overhang.
12. Tip the cheese and spinach filling into the pastry.
13. Roll out the remaining 1/3 pastry until it is big enough to be used as the pie lid and put on top.
14. Crimp the pie lid to the edges of the pie using the back of a fork to press the edges together.
15. If there is any pasty left, decorate the top.
16. Using a knife, put a slit in the middle of the top of the pie to allow steam to escape.
17. Chill in the fridge for least 20 minutes.
18. Brush the pastry top with the beaten egg.
19. Bake in the oven at 170°C for 30 minutes, until golden brown.
20. Serve with potatoes and seasonal vegetables.

Sea Bass en Papillote

'Papillote' simply means cooking in a paper bag. This method has many benefits as the paper bag traps in the steam which helps to retain the juices and flavours, resulting in a more succulent and flavourful fish.

This dish lists herb butters as part of the ingredients. These are so easy to make yourself, the recipe for which is on page 31.

Ingredients:

- 1 sea bass, filleted and sliced in half
- 150ml of double cream
- 50g of parsley butter
- 50g of tarragon butter
- 8 tarragon leaves
- 1 clove of garlic, peeled and finely chopped
- Salt - for seasoning
- Ground black pepper - for seasoning
- 150ml of white wine

Method:
1. Cut a piece of greaseproof paper to size so that it is twice the size of the sea bass.
2. Lay both halves of the sea bass on the baking parchment, scales side down. On one half of the fish, spread the parsley butter into the flesh and also sprinkle the salt and pepper.
3. Place the other sea bass back on top so that the fish is whole again.
4. Pour six teaspoons of the white wine onto the fish and then wrap the greaseproof paper around it like a parcel. Leave the rest of the white wine for later.
5. Put the fish on a baking tray and cook in the oven at 170ºC for 12 minutes whilst you make the sauce.
6. In a saucepan add the tarragon butter and the garlic and cook for 2 minutes.
7. Add the tarragon leaves and the white wine and cook until the liquid has reduced by half.
8. Add the double cream and season with salt and black pepper.
9. Simmer for 5 minutes.
10. Serve the sea bass with a drizzle of the cream sauce and seasonal vegetables.

Coconut Fish Curry

Coconut fish curry is beautiful fusion of Thai and Indian cuisine, making a dish vibrant in colour, taste and aroma. For those of you who are not fond of spicy curries, this recipe is perfect as the spices are very subtle and the coconut milk makes it so delicate and creamy.

Ingredients:

- 1 small cod (or another whitefish such as halibut or hake), deboned and cut into 3cm chunks
- 350g of tiger prawns
- 1 white onion, peeled and finely chopped
- The juice of 1/2 a lime
- A 60g bunch of fresh coriander, finely chopped
- 3 stalks of lemongrass
- 3 garlic cloves, peeled and finely chopped
- 2cm of ginger root, peeled and finely chopped
- 2 small red chillies, finely chopped
- 2 teaspoons of medium heat curry powder
- 1 teaspoon of shrimp paste

- 1 tablespoon of light muscovado sugar
- A 400ml tin of coconut milk
- 1 tablespoon of vegetable oil

Method:

1. Heat the vegetable oil in a large frying pan and add the onion slices, cooking for 5 minutes until they have softened.
2. Prepare the lemongrass by removing and discarding the outer leaves and the bulb end. Bruise the lemongrass by making several superficial cuts along the length of it, then hold it at either end and gently bend the lemongrass (this will release more of the flavour).
3. Increase the heat a little and stir in the garlic, ginger, chillies, lemongrass and the shrimp paste for 2 minutes.
4. Add the curry powder and the muscovado sugar and keep stirring.
5. When the sugar has melted, you should be able to feel the mixture starting to clump together when you stir. At this stage, add the coconut milk and one half of the coriander.

Listen out for the heat of the pan, ensuring it is simmering and not boiling.

6. Add the cod and the prawns to the pan as well as half of the lime juice.
7. Cover with a lid and simmer for a further 5 minutes. You will know when the cod is cooked by touching it with a fork where it should slightly flake.
8. Season with salt and extra lime juice if required.
9. Garnish with the remaining coriander and serve.

Slow-Roasted Pork Shoulder

This dish has long marinade and cooking time, but trust me, it is worth the wait. There is nothing more succulent and tender than slow-roasted pork that has been extensively marinated.

Ingredients:
- 1.5kg of pork shoulder, deboned
- 2 teaspoons of coarse sea salt
- 2 teaspoons of barbecue seasoning powder
- 4 teaspoons of smoked paprika powder
- 1 teaspoon of ground cumin
- 1 teaspoon of mustard powder
- 1/4 teaspoon of chilli powder
- 1 tablespoon of black treacle
- 3 teaspoons of cider vinegar
- 100ml of cider

Method:
1. In a mixing bowl, create a marinade by mixing the black treacle, cider vinegar, smoked paprika, barbecue seasoning, cumin, mustard and chilli powder.

2. Make slashes in the top of the pork shoulder where the smooth layer of fat is. Make the slashes deep enough to cut through the layer of fat but not the actual meat itself.
3. Turn the shoulder over and rub the marinade primarily into the meat (not the fat).
4. Chill in the fridge for at least 24 hours to marinate.
5. After 24 hours, rub the coarse sea salt on to the fat of the pork, deep into the slashes.
6. In a large roasting dish, place a wire rack and put the pork shoulder on top of the wire rack with the fat layer facing up.
7. Pour 300ml of water and 100ml of cider into the bottom of the roasting tin (underneath the wire rack).
8. Cover the pork loosely with foil and cook in the oven at 140°C for 4 hours.
9. After 4 hours, remove the foil, turn the oven up to 180°C and cook for a further 45 minutes until the pork is very tender and the skin has a crispy crackling.
10. Once the pork is tender, remove from the oven, cover with foil and leave to rest.

11. Pour the juice from the roasting tin into a jug and leave to settle and separate. There will be a thick fat layer in the jug which you can skim and discard. I have found the best VI method to do this is to pour the jug slowly and very carefully into another jug, where the fat will leave the jug first, leaving the required juice last.
12. With the remaining liquid, place it into a saucepan, simmering on a high heat until it has been reduced. Add the cider and boil until the liquid has reduced again.
13. Serve the pork with the liquid drizzled on top as well as seasonal vegetables.

Duck Breast with Apple Pave

A real showstopper of a main course, containing lots of elements that come together perfectly. I have always found duck and apple to be an underrated partnership as the flavours really do go well together.

Ingredients:
- 2 duck breasts
- 50g of butter
- 500ml of milk
- 200ml of double cream
- 3 Granny Smith apples, peeled and sliced into rounds
- 3 Pink Lady apples, peeled and sliced into rounds
- 1 celeriac, peeled and diced
- 50g of walnuts, chopped
- 1/2 teaspoon of salt
- 3 tablespoons of ground cinnamon
- 6 tablespoons of light brown sugar
- 1 tablespoon of maple syrup
- 2 vegetable stock cubes
- 200ml of red wine

Method:

1. Melt the butter in a pan, and set aside.
2. Peel, core and slice the Granny Smith and Pink Lady apples into circles, patting the apples dry with a kitchen towel.
3. Cover an oven baking tray with greaseproof paper and put a layer of apple circles on to it, saving enough for another a layer later.
4. Brush the apples with the melted butter and sprinkle with light brown sugar and the cinnamon.
5. Use the remaining apples to put another layer on top.
6. Cook in the oven at 160°C for 2 hours.
7. Leaving the apples on the tray, allow to cool and then place another piece of greaseproof paper on top, followed by a heavy object to crush the apples.
8. Put the tray (including the item of weight), into the fridge.
9. Place the peeled and diced celeriac into a pan, adding the salt, milk and double cream, boiling until it feels soft.
10. Blitz the mixture until it is a smooth purée and set aside.

11. In a different saucepan, add the stock cubes (dissolved in 200ml of water), as well as the red wine and maple syrup, boiling until it has been reduced to a thick syrup which feels thick to stir. Set aside.
12. Place the duck in a frying pan and over a low heat, slowly brown the duck on both sides.
13. Place the duck on a baking tray in the oven and turn up to 180°C, cooking the duck for 7 minutes.
14. Leave the duck to rest for 12 minutes.
15. On a serving plate, fan out the apple pave and place the duck breast on top.
16. On top of the duck breast, drizzle the maple syrup mixture as well as the walnuts.
17. Serve with the celeriac purée and seasonal vegetables.

Beef Wellington

Not much beats this British classic with its beautifully tender fillet encased in golden, crispy puff pastry. This recipe also includes the traditional pâté filling, creating a luxuriously rich dish.

Ingredients:
- 1kg of beef fillet (the middle section)
- 140g of chicken liver pâté
- 100g of butter
- 2 eggs, beaten - for the pancake
- 3 egg yolks, beaten
- 180ml of milk
- A 320g packet of ready-rolled puff pastry (one sheet)
- 150g of wild mushrooms, finely chopped
- 4 portobello mushrooms, finely chopped
- 120g of baby spinach
- Salt - for seasoning
- Ground black pepper - for seasoning
- 60g of plain flour
- 1 beef stock cube
- 1 teaspoon of olive oil
- 70ml of red wine

Method:

1. Heat the olive oil in a frying pan on a high heat.
2. Add the beef fillet and fry until it has seared and the flesh feels firm.
3. Wrap the beef fillet very tightly in a large piece of kitchen foil to form a cylinder shape, twisting the ends of the foil to secure it in place.
4. Chill in the fridge for 1 hour.
5. In a frying pan, melt one quarter of the butter over a medium heat.
6. Add the portobello mushrooms and fry for 2 minutes until they have softened. Transfer the mushrooms into a bowl, patting them with a kitchen towel until the excess moisture has gone.
7. In the same frying pan, add another quarter of the butter and fry the spinach for 30 seconds until it starts to wilt and you can feel it reduce in volume.
8. Transfer the spinach to a plate and set aside.
9. Place the two beaten eggs and flour into a mixing bowl and whisk together.

10. Gradually whisk the milk in until it becomes a smooth batter which is thick enough to coat the back of a spoon.
11. In a hot frying pan, add another quarter of the butter.
12. When the butter starts smoking, add a ladle full of the pancake batter, swirling it around the frying pan so that covers the full area and evenly coats the base.
13. Fry for 2 minutes until the underside of the pancake is firm to the touch and golden brown in colour.
14. Flip the pancake and cook the other side until that too is firm and golden brown.
15. When done, place the pancake on a layer of greaseproof paper. You will need approximately four pancakes to cover the beef, so repeat.
16. Roll out the puff pastry on a lightly floured worktop until it is big enough to wrap the beef fillet in later.
17. Cover the centre of the pastry with the pancakes.

18. Spread the chicken liver pâté evenly over the pancakes.
19. Place the wilted spinach on top and season with salt and black pepper.
20. Unwrap the beef fillet from the foil and place on top of the spinach.
21. Brush some of the beaten egg yolks around the edges of the pastry border. Then tightly roll the pastry ensuring all the sides are sealed.
22. Place the Wellington on a baking tray with the seam side down.
23. Chill in the fridge for 2 hours.
24. Take the Wellington out of the fridge and brush with the remaining beaten egg yolks.
25. Bake the Wellington in the oven at 180°C for 35 minutes or until the pastry feels crisp.
26. Heat the last quarter of butter in a frying pan over high heat and add the wild mushrooms, frying for 3 minutes.
27. Add the red wine and boil for 3 minutes.
28. Add the beef stock (dissolved in 300ml of water), bring to the boil again and then reduce the heat and simmer until 1/3 of the liquid has gone.

29. Serve the Wellington with this liquid drizzled on top as well as seasonal vegetables.

Desserts

Hints & Tips

- I always use unsalted butter. For me, the difference in taste between butter and margarine is worth the calories.
- If using an oven, I always preheat the oven first. Never put a cake into a cold oven.
- Always sift the flour. Doing this makes the cakes light.
- Flour should always be folded into the batter as this helps to trap the air in the mixture, which again, helps to make the cake lighter.
- Cakes are sensitive. When they are in the oven, don't be tempted to check on them too early (before three quarters of the baking time) as opening the oven door too early will cause the cakes to droop and drop in the middle.
- Different ovens and different brands of ingredients will affect the baking times.

I always check my cakes 5 minutes before the required time, and then every 5 minutes after that to see if they are done.

- A good method to check that a cake is done is to touch the top where it should feel firm and not wobblily. If you have sight, you will be able to see that the cake will also start to come away from the sides of the tin too. However, I have found the best way to check whether a cake is done is to use a skewer or a sharp knife in the centre of the cake. If the utensil comes out dry with no cake batter on, then the cake is done. Please be aware though, that if you are baking with fruit in the mixture, there may be some stickiness on the knife/skewer which is fine as long as there is no cake batter present.

Lemon Drizzle Cake

Of all the cakes and bakes that I do, a classic lemon drizzle is probably one of my favourites for its zesty, fresh taste. Complimenting the lemon flavour is a generous layer of raspberry jam in between the two sponges, creating a cake that is utter perfection. For a retro twist, serve warm with lashings of custard.

Ingredients:
- 280g of unsalted butter
- 5 large eggs, beaten
- The zest and juice of 2 lemons
- 280g of self-raising flour
- 280g of caster sugar
- 200g of icing sugar
- 1 teaspoon of lemon extract
- 100g of raspberry jam

Method:

1. Preheat the oven to 170°C.

2. Prepare two 18cm cake tins by lining them with greaseproof baking paper and a thin layer of butter on the base and sides.

3. In a mixing bowl, cream the butter and the caster sugar until light and creamy. Also add the lemon extract and lemon zest at this stage.

4. Very slowly, drizzle the beaten eggs into the mixing bowl and whisk until fluffy. If the mixture feels as though it is about to curdle, add a tablespoon of flour.

5. Fold in the flour using a spoon.

6. Divide the mixture into the two cake tins and bake in the oven for 25 minutes. Do not open the oven before this as the cakes will collapse in on themselves.

7. After 25 minutes, check to see if the cakes are done by feeling the top. The top should feel firm. Also, pierce the centre of the cakes with a knife or a skewer. If the knife comes out clean, the cakes are done.

8. When done, take the cakes out of the tins and leave to cool.

9. When the cakes have cooled, slice the top off one of the cakes so that the surface is completely flat.
10. Add the raspberry jam to this surface and then place the other cake on top.
11. Put the icing sugar into a mixing bowl and add the juice of the lemons, mixing until it becomes runny, the consistency of double cream. If the mixture is too thick and there is no lemon juice left, just add a little water.
12. With a skewer, put a few holes in the top of the cake and pour the lemon flavoured icing over the top.
13. Leave to set for 30 minutes.
14. Slice into thick slices and serve with custard.

Cherry Cake

One of my daughter's favourites, it is not hard to understand why the humble cherry cake is considered a British classic. There is nothing nicer than a traditional cake accompanied by bursts of sweet and juicy glacè cherries. This recipe is so easy and simple to make too.

Ingredients:
- 3 large eggs, beaten
- 3 tablespoons of milk
- 175g of unsalted butter
- 350g of glacè cherries, cut into halves
- 300g of self-raising flour
- 200g of caster sugar
- 50g of ground almonds
- 1 teaspoon of vanilla extract

Method:

1. Preheat the oven to 170°C.
2. Prepare an 18cm cake tin by lining it with greaseproof baking paper and a thin layer of butter on the base and sides.
3. In a mixing bowl, cream the butter and the caster sugar until light and creamy. Also add the vanilla extract at this stage.
4. Very slowly, drizzle the beaten eggs into the mixing bowl and whisk until fluffy. If the mixture feels as though it is about to curdle, add a tablespoon of flour.
5. Spread the glacè cherries on a plate and dust them with flour (approximately two tablespoons worth).
6. Into the batter, fold in the remaining flour using a spoon.
7. Add the glacè cherries, ground almonds and the milk, making sure that the cherries are mixed evenly in the mixture.
8. Put the mixture into the cake tin and sprinkle the top of it with one teaspoon of cold water.
9. Bake in the oven for 20 minutes. Do not open the oven before this as the cake will collapse in on itself.

10. After 20 minutes, check to see if the cake is done by feeling the top. The top should feel firm. Also, pierce the centre of the cake with a knife or a skewer. If the knife comes out clean, the cake is done. There may be some stickiness on the knife/skewer from the glacè cherries, but there should be no batter present.

11. When done, take the cake out of the tin and leave to cool.

12. Slice into thick slices and serve.

Apple & Cinnamon Cake

Apple and cinnamon, what a perfect partnering; the crispness of the apple complimented by the warmth of the cinnamon. With juicy chunks of apple in every bite, this has to be amongst one of my favourite bakes.

Ingredients:
- 5 large eggs, beaten
- 280g of unsalted butter
- 3 Granny Smith apples
- 3 Pink Lady apples
- The juice of a lemon
- 280g of self-raising flour
- 280g of caster sugar
- 100g of icing sugar
- 2 teaspoons of vanilla extract
- 3 teaspoons of cinnamon powder

Method:

1. Preheat the oven to 170°C.

2. Prepare an 18cm cake tin by lining it with greaseproof baking paper and a thin layer of butter on the base and sides.

3. In a mixing bowl, cream the butter and the caster sugar until light and creamy. Also add the cinnamon powder and vanilla extract at this stage.

4. Very slowly, drizzle the beaten eggs into the mixing bowl and whisk until fluffy. If the mixture feels as though it is about to curdle, add a tablespoon of flour.

5. Peel and core the Granny Smith and Pink Lady apples. Then chop them into 1cm cubes. To avoid the apples browning through exposure to the air, once chopped, put them into a mixing bowl full of cold water and one tablespoon of lemon juice.

6. Drain the apples, spread them on a plate and dust them with flour (approximately two tablespoons worth).

7. In the mixing bowl, fold in the remaining flour using a spoon.

8. Add the apple cubes, making sure they are spread evenly in the mixture.
9. Put the mixture into the cake tin and bake in the oven for 30 minutes. Do not open the oven before this as the cake will collapse in on itself.
10. After 30 minutes, check to see if the cake is done by feeling the top. The top should feel firm. Also, pierce the centre of the cake with a knife or a skewer. If the knife comes out clean, the cake is done. There may be some stickiness on the knife/skewer from the apples, but there should be no batter present.
11. When done, take the cake out of the tin and leave to cool.
12. When the cake has cooled, put the icing sugar into a mixing bowl and add the juice of the lemon, mixing it until it becomes runny, the consistency of double cream. If the mixture is too thick and there is no lemon juice left, just add a little water.
13. Pour the lemon flavoured icing over the top of the cake and leave to set for 30 minutes.
14. Slice into thick slices and serve.

Chocolate Espresso Cheesecake

This is one of my favourite cheesecake recipes. Not only is it luxuriously indulgent, it is easy to make with no baking necessary. It has a delicious base comprising of a heavenly mix of digestive and gingernut biscuits, and a light and fluffy cheesecake topping. A delightful dessert to add to anyone's culinary repertoire.

Ingredients:
- 360g of cream cheese
- 500ml of double cream
- 135g of unsalted butter - for the crumb base
- 10g of unsalted butter - for the melted chocolate
- 150g of gingernut biscuits
- 100g of digestive biscuits
- 230g of dark chocolate (at least 70% cocoa)
- 25g of white chocolate
- 2 teaspoons of instant coffee
- 1 tablespoon of rum (optional)

Method:

1. Prepare an 18cm cake tin by lining it with greaseproof baking paper and a thin layer of butter on the base and the lower third of the sides. A springform cake tin is recommended for this cheesecake.

2. In a saucepan or a microwave, melt the 135g of butter until it becomes a liquid with no lumps.

3. In a food processor, blitz the gingernut and digestive biscuits until they are ground down into crumbs.

4. In a mixing bowl, mix together the biscuit crumbs with the melted butter.

5. Press the mixture into the cake tin, compacting it by pushing down on the mixture with the back of a large spoon to create a sturdy base.

6. Chill the cake tin in the fridge for at least 3 hours (but ideally overnight).

7. Melt the dark chocolate by breaking it into pieces and putting it in a glass bowl (along with the 10g of butter) over a pan of boiling water on the hob. Stir continuously until you

can feel that the chocolate and butter have melted.

8. Add the coffee and the rum to the chocolate and leave to cool.

9. In a separate mixing bowl, add the double cream and whisk until it feels thicker.

10. Stir in the cream cheese until thoroughly mixed.

11. Fold in the melted chocolate until thoroughly mixed.

12. Put the mixture on top of the biscuit base and chill in the fridge overnight for the cheesecake to set.

13. The next day, remove the cheesecake from the tin. You may need to run a knife along the edges of the tin as the cheesecake may cling to the sides.

14. Decorate the cheesecake by grating the white chocolate on top of it. You can even use a potato peeler to do this if you prefer larger curls.

15. Slice into thick slices and serve.

Pecan Pie

Pecan pie is a traditional all-American dessert, native to the southern states. It is understandably a very popular dessert. It is usually made with sweet shortcrust pastry, but if you don't have much of a sweet tooth, this can be substituted for ordinary shortcrust.

Ingredients:
- 1 large egg yolk, beaten - for the shortcrust pastry
- 3 large eggs, beaten
- 75g of unsalted butter - for the shortcrust pastry
- 30g of unsalted butter - for the mixture
- 200g of pecan halves
- 175g of plain flour - for the shortcrust pastry
- 175g of muscovado sugar
- 15g of icing sugar - for the shortcrust pastry
- 200ml of maple syrup
- 1 teaspoon of vanilla extract

Method:
1. To make the shortcrust pastry, in a mixing bowl, add the flour and the icing sugar.
2. Add the 75g of butter to this and rub until it feels like breadcrumbs.
3. Add one beaten egg yolk and one tablespoon of cold water and mix until it becomes a soft dough. If necessary, add more water.
4. Wrap the dough in cling film and chill in the fridge for at least 1 hour.
5. Prepare a 20cm flan/tart dish by lining it with greaseproof baking paper and a thin layer of butter on the base and sides.
6. Roll out the pastry onto a floured work surface/board until it is approximately 3mm thick.
7. Gently put the pastry over the dish, pressing down the edges and leaving a 2cm overhang.
8. Chill the pie base in the fridge for 30 minutes.
9. Preheat the oven to 170°C.
10. In a mixing bowl, cream the 30g of butter and the muscovado sugar until light and creamy. Also add the maple syrup and vanilla extract at this stage.

11. Very slowly, drizzle the beaten eggs into the mixing bowl and whisk until fluffy.
12. Before putting this into the flan dish, arrange half of the pecan halves on top of the pastry.
13. Then pour the mixture into the flan dish.
14. Arrange the remaining pecan halves on top.
15. Bake in the oven for 30 minutes or until the pie feels firm to the touch.
16. Slice into thick slices and serve with whipped cream or vanilla ice cream.

Carrot Cake

This particular carrot cake recipe is an old 1950's recipe which I have adapted and tweaked. Replacing the butter with vegetable oil makes for an incredibly moist and moreish cake that perfectly accompanies the sweetness of the carrots.

Ingredients:
- 3 large eggs, beaten
- 340g of carrots, peeled and finely grated
- The zest and juice of 2 oranges
- 225g of plain flour
- 225g of caster sugar
- 180g of icing sugar
- 1/2 teaspoon of salt
- 3 teaspoons of cinnamon powder
- 2 teaspoons of vanilla extract
- 1/2 teaspoon of baking powder
- 1 teaspoon of bicarbonate of soda
- 3/4 of a mug of vegetable oil

Method:

1. Preheat the oven to 170°C.
2. Prepare a large, deep rectangular oven tray by lining it with greaseproof baking paper and a thin coating of vegetable oil on the base and sides (removing the excess oil with a piece of kitchen roll).
3. In a mixing bowl, add the caster sugar, oil, vanilla extract and the beaten eggs, whisking for at least 5 minutes until you can feel the mixture thicken, increased in volume. It should be the consistency of double cream.
4. Fold in the flour, bicarbonate of soda, salt, cinnamon, baking powder and the grated carrots with a spoon.
5. Put the mixture into the deep oven tray and bake in the oven for 25 minutes. Do not open the oven before this as the cake will collapse in on itself.
6. After 25 minutes, check to see if the cake is done by feeling the top. The top should feel firm. Also, pierce the centre of the cake with a knife or a skewer. If the knife comes out clean, the cake is done.

7. When done, take the cake out of the tray and leave to cool.
8. When the cake has cooled, put the icing sugar into a mixing bowl and add the juice and the zest of the oranges, mixing until it becomes runny, the consistency of double cream. If the mixture is too thick and there is no orange juice left, just add a little water.
9. With a skewer, put a few holes in the top of the cake and pour the orange flavoured icing over the top.
10. Leave to set for 30 minutes.
11. Slice into chunky squares and serve with clotted cream.

Orangecello Bites

A recipe native to Germany, this is a beautifully layered dessert consisting of three distinctive layers; a light cocoa sponge base, a fluffy cheesecake middle and a juicy topping. It is the perfect summery dessert that is guaranteed to impress and so fun to make too.

Ingredients:
- 5 medium eggs, beaten
- 100g of unsalted butter
- 100ml of double cream
- 750g of cream cheese
- 150g of caster sugar - for the sponge mixture
- 90g of caster sugar - for the jelly topping
- 150g of icing sugar
- 150g of self-raising flour
- 1/4 teaspoon of salt
- 80g of cornflour
- 55g of cocoa powder
- 1 teaspoon of vanilla extract
- 800ml of orange juice
- 50ml of vegetable oil

Method:

1. Preheat the oven to 170°C.
2. Prepare a large, deep rectangular oven tray by lining it with greaseproof baking paper and a thin coating of vegetable oil on the base (removing the excess oil with a piece of kitchen roll).
3. In a mixing bowl, put the 150g of caster sugar, salt and the beaten eggs together and whisk for at least 4 minutes until the mixture feels fluffy.
4. Add the vegetable oil and mix for another minute.
5. Fold in the flour and the cocoa powder using a spoon.
6. Put the mixture into the deep oven tray and bake for 15 minutes.
7. After 15 minutes, check to see if the cake layer is done by feeling it. It should feel firm. Also, pierce the centre of the cake layer with a knife or a skewer. If the knife comes out clean, the cake layer is done.
8. When done, leave the cake layer in the tray and set aside to cool.

9. When the cake has cooled, put the double cream into a mixing bowl and whisk until it feels thicker.
10. Put the cream cheese into the mixing bowl and stir until it is thoroughly mixed.
11. Add the icing sugar, vanilla extract and the softened butter, mixing for another minute.
12. Put the mixture on top of the cooled sponge base in the tray and gently smooth until flat.
13. Chill in the fridge for 1 hour until the cheesecake layer feels firmer.
14. In a saucepan, over a low/medium heat, add the orange juice, cornflour and the 90g of caster sugar.
15. Stir frequently until you can feel the consistency changing from a smooth liquid to a thick pudding mixture.
16. When it has reached a thick consistency, remove from the heat and let it cool down.
17. When it has cooled down entirely, add to the top of the cheesecake mixture in the tray and gently smooth the surface.
18. Chill in the fridge for 3 hours until it has set.
19. Slice into neat squares to reveal the layers and serve.

Chocolate Biscuit Cake

When my kids were little, they loved this rich chocolate biscuit cake. And like most kids, there was always more chocolate on their cheeky little faces than actually in the mixing bowl!

Ingredients:
- 125g of unsalted butter - for the mixture
- 15g of unsalted butter - for the melted chocolate
- 2 tablespoons of milk
- 50g of raisins
- 50g of glace cherries, cut into halves
- 50g of caster sugar
- 2 tablespoons of golden syrup
- 2 tablespoons of drinking chocolate
- 125g of dark chocolate (at least 70% cocoa)
- 3 tablespoons of cocoa powder
- 250g of digestive biscuits

Method:
1. Prepare a 20cm flan/tart dish by lining it with greaseproof baking paper and a thin layer of butter on the base and sides.

2. In a saucepan, add the caster sugar, golden syrup, milk and the 125g of unsalted butter and heat gently on a low heat, listening to ensure the saucepan is just simmering and not vigorously boiling.
3. In a food processor, blitz the biscuits until they are ground down into crumbs and then transfer them to a mixing bowl.
4. In the same mixing bowl, add the drinking chocolate, cocoa powder, glace cherries, raisins and mix well.
5. Press the mixture into the tart dish, compacting it by pushing down on the mixture with the back of a large spoon to create a sturdy base.
6. Chill in the fridge for at least 1 hour, until it feels firm to the touch.
7. Melt the dark chocolate by breaking it into pieces and putting it in a glass bowl (along with the 15g of butter) over a pan of boiling water on the hob. Stir continuously until the chocolate and butter have melted.
8. Cool for 1 minute and then pour the mixture on top of the tart and leave it to cool and set.
9. Slice into thick slices and serve.

Tiramisu Torte

This elegant dessert is a fabulous indulgence of coffee and chocolate, the perfect ending to a special meal. To offset the richness of the torte, I always serve this dessert with clotted cream which compliments it beautifully.

Ingredients:
- 3 large eggs, with the yolks and whites separated
- 75g of unsalted butter
- 700g of cream cheese
- 25g of plain flour
- 150g of caster sugar
- 275g of amaretti biscuits (or macaroons)
- 1 teaspoon of vanilla extract
- 175g of dark chocolate (at least 70% cocoa)
- 1 tablespoon of ground coffee
- 3 tablespoons of dark rum
- 3 tablespoons of Tia Maria (or any other coffee liqueur)

Method:

1. Prepare a 20cm flan/tart dish by lining it with greaseproof baking paper and a thin layer of butter on the base and the lower third of the sides.
2. In a saucepan or a microwave, melt the butter until it becomes a liquid with no lumps.
3. In a food processor, blitz the amaretti biscuits until they are ground down into crumbs.
4. In a mixing bowl, mix together the biscuit crumbs with the melted butter and mix thoroughly.
5. Press the mixture into the tart dish, compacting it by pushing down on the mixture with the back of a large spoon to create a sturdy base.
6. Chill the tart dish in the fridge for at least 1 hour.
7. Pre-heat the oven to 180°C.
8. In a mixing bowl, add the cream cheese, sugar and egg yolks and whisk until smooth.
9. Fold in the flour with a spoon.
10. Divide this cake mixture into two bowls.

11. In one of the cake mixtures, add the vanilla extract and dark rum and set aside.
12. Melt the dark chocolate by breaking it into pieces and putting it in a glass bowl over a pan of boiling water on the hob. Stir continuously until the chocolate has melted.
13. Add the coffee and the coffee liqueur to the chocolate and leave to cool for 2 minutes.
14. Add this chocolate mixture to the second half of the cake mixture (the half that hasn't got the vanilla and rum in).
15. In another mixing bowl, whisk the egg whites until you can feel that they are starting to form soft peaks.
16. Divide the egg whites into two, and then quickly (but gently) fold in the egg whites to each half of the cake mixtures set aside earlier.
17. Spoon alternate mounds of the two cake mixtures into the biscuit base until it is full.
18. Using a knife or a skewer, make swirling, figure of eight movements in the mixture for a marbled effect when it is cut into later.
19. Bake in the oven for 40 minutes, covering with foil if it appears to be over-browning.

20. After 40 minutes, the centre should be soft in the middle but not liquid. At this stage, leave the cake to cool in the switched off oven, with the door slightly ajar.
21. Once firmed, take out of the oven and leave to cool.
22. Chill in the fridge for several hours.
23. Slice and serve with clotted cream.

Chocolate Brownies

A must for chocoholics, chocolate brownies are the ultimate indulgent treat, the richness of the chocolate (especially when it is at least 70% cocoa) complimenting the sweetness of the batter. I cannot begin to describe the heavenly aroma of these brownies, lingering in my home for days afterwards. They are a real treat.

Ingredients:
- 3 large eggs, beaten
- 185g of unsalted butter
- 260g of caster sugar
- 1 tablespoon of icing sugar
- 185g of dark chocolate (at least 70% cocoa)
- 50g of raspberry flavoured white or dark chocolate, chopped roughly into 1cm pieces
- 40g of cocoa powder
- 85g of plain flour
- 1 tablespoon of dark rum

Method:

1. Preheat the oven to 170°C.
2. Prepare a large, deep rectangular oven tray by lining it with greaseproof baking paper and a thin layer of butter on the base and sides.
3. Melt the 185g of dark chocolate by breaking it into pieces and putting it in a glass bowl (along with the 185g of butter) over a pan of boiling water on the hob. Stir continuously until the chocolate and butter have melted. Put aside to cool slightly.
4. In a mixing bowl, cream the beaten eggs and the caster sugar until fluffy.
5. Fold in the flour and the cocoa powder using a spoon.
6. Roughly chop the 50g of raspberry chocolate into small pieces (approximately 1cm in size) and add this to the mixing bowl.
7. Add the melted chocolate mixture as well as the rum to the mixing bowl.
8. Transfer to a deep oven tray and bake in the oven for 20 minutes. Do not open the oven before this as the brownie tray bake will collapse in on itself.

9. After 20 minutes, check to see if the brownies are done by feeling the top. The top should feel firm. Also, pierce the centre of the brownies with a knife or a skewer. Brownies are generally a little stickier than a normal cake mixture so the knife/skewer may not be completely clean, just as long as it is not too runny.
10. When done, take the brownie tray bake out of the tray and leave to cool.
11. Dust the top of the tray bake with a fine layer of icing sugar, slice into chunky squares and serve.

Coffee Cake

Is any recipe book complete without a decadent coffee cake? This recipe is the perfect blend of coffee and vanilla, each subtly enhancing one another. Made in a loaf tin, it can be easily sliced and shared (if you're feeling generous of course).

Ingredients:
- 3 medium eggs, beaten
- 175g of unsalted butter
- 175g of golden caster sugar
- 175g of icing sugar
- 175 of self-raising flour
- 1 teaspoon of vanilla extract
- 1/4 teaspoon of baking powder
- 3 teaspoons of instant coffee dissolved in 1 tablespoon of boiling water
- 1 teaspoon of Tia Maria (or any other coffee liqueur)
- 4 tablespoons of rum

Method:

1. Preheat the oven to 170°C.
2. Prepare a 24cm loaf tin by lining it with greaseproof baking paper and a thin layer of butter on the base and sides.
3. In a mixing bowl, cream the butter and the golden caster sugar until fluffy. Please note, as you are using golden caster sugar rather than normal caster sugar, there will be a little bit of a gritty texture (this is normal).
4. Very slowly, drizzle the beaten eggs into the mixing bowl and whisk until fluffy.
5. Fold in the flour and baking powder using a spoon.
6. Divide the mixture into 2 bowls.
7. In one of the bowls, fold in the vanilla extract.
8. In the other half of the mixture, add the concentrated coffee (3 teaspoons of coffee mixed with 1 tablespoon of boiling water) and the coffee liqueur.
9. Pour the mixture containing the coffee liqueur into the loaf tin, followed by the vanilla flavoured mixture on top.

10. Using a knife or a skewer, make swirling, figure of eight movements in the mixture for a marbled effect when it is cut into later.
11. Bake in the oven for 20 minutes. Do not open the oven before this as the cake will collapse in on itself.
12. After 20 minutes, check to see if the cake is done by feeling the top. The top should feel firm. Also, pierce the centre of the cake with a knife or a skewer. If the knife comes out clean, the cake is done. I have found that with this cake, the mixture can be liquid until the very last 5 or 7 minutes, so after 20 minutes, keep checking every 5 minutes to see if it has set.
13. When done, take the cake out of the loaf tin and leave to cool.
14. When the cake has cooled, put the icing sugar into a mixing bowl and add the rum, mixing it until it becomes runny, the consistency of double cream.
15. Pour the rum flavoured icing over the top of the cake and leave to set for 30 minutes.
16. Slice into thick slices and serve.

Butterscotch Pudding

Nothing ends a meal like a big bowl of pudding and butterscotch pudding in particular always takes me back to my school days. For the full nostalgic experience, serve hot with lashings of custard. Butterscotch pudding is the perfect comfort food and so simple to make. A real family favourite.

Ingredients:
- 3 large eggs, beaten
- 100g of unsalted butter
- 250ml of milk
- 140g of light brown sugar - for the sponge mixture
- 160g of light brown sugar - for the caramel/golden syrup sauce
- 275g of self-raising flour
- 1 teaspoon of baking powder
- 2 tablespoons of golden syrup
- 4 tablespoons of caramel carnation milk

Method:

1. Preheat the oven to 170°C.
2. Prepare a large, deep rectangular oven tray by lining it with greaseproof baking paper and a thin layer of butter on the base and sides.
3. In a mixing bowl, put the butter, milk and beaten eggs together and whisk.
4. Fold in the flour, baking powder, a pinch of salt and 140g of light brown sugar using a spoon.
5. Put the mixture into the deep oven tray and set aside.
6. In a mixing bowl, add the remaining 160g of light brown sugar, golden syrup and caramel carnation milk.
7. Add 300ml of boiling water and stir until the ingredients have dissolved.
8. Pour the hot liquid over the mixture in the deep oven tray, set aside earlier.
9. Bake in the oven for 50 minutes or until the top feels firm.
10. Don't set aside to cool. Slice into chunky squares and serve immediately whilst hot with custard or double cream.

Printed in Great Britain
by Amazon